Hey, Think Big... Be Big... with the top 3 health sites for Hardcore films and your very own Alhocol Keychain Breath Tester – Amazing!

Attention Business Owners: Acquire Debt Relief with Raunchy love stories about Spanish painter GOYA Y LUCIENTES (1746-1828) and you'll be able to earn $2000 DAILY OR WEEKLY RETURNING PHONE CALLS. We Can All Handle Various situations so don't worry – they told us you were very small. They won't laugh anymore.

Do you have septic problems? Attain a school diploma rapidly without Pills, Pumps or Surgery. We serve over 18 here so Turn Back Your Biological Clock.

Are you MAD that mother nature cheated you? Guess what?!? The Lowest Just Got Lower. If you click here, you can see the profiles of a single woman and find Summer love. Why don't you like it? Please don't tell her – just become an addict and your problems will be solved! If you want bigger jugs, you'll need reasonable dental coverage. So check out this weeks issue... ***this should wake you up!***

Rick Smith
http://www.ufoteacher.com/

ABOUT THE AUTHOR

Since 1991, Rick has been 'downloading' extraterrestrial information, turning it into visual and literary expressions throughout his work as an artist, poet and lecturer. His exploration into this realm began with acrylics. As time went on, the natural evolution of this exploration led him down the path of a mixed-media artist, writer and lecturer. In *Legions Of Light / Armies Of Darkness* he exposes his own intimate, enlightening and horrific experiences, scenarios and confrontations for the first time. As a teacher of the masses and a relentless truth machine, Rick Smith knows his calling in life as he redeems the Abduction Phenomenon away from falsehood, delivering unto the viewer a message of catalystic knowledge. Ranging in areas of politics, religion, domestic violence and sociological evolution, the far reaching implications set forth by the artist's work become startling and hard hitting.